Gaines

Gaines

WHAT
and
WHAT-NOT

A PICTURE STORY OF ART
BY KAY PETERSON PARKER

HOUGHTON MIFFLIN COMPANY
BOSTON ——————————————— 1944

CC

Where (so far as is known) the works of art pictured in this book can be found today:

Acknowledgment is made to the museums and collectors as listed.

Uncle Andrew, who was an architect, didn't like the
Cape Cod house in New Jersey where John and Lucy lived. It was a fine
house, he said, for the people on Cape Cod who first built one like it way
back in 1630. But it wasn't at all
the kind of house to live in today
when life is altogether different.

And he didn't like Grandmother's house any better. This house had been built for Grandmother's father in 1880 when she was ten years old. *She* liked it very much and she didn't care for Uncle Andrew's newfangled houses at all. *He* said that was because Grandmother grew up in the "Whatnot Age."

A Whatnot

When John and Lucy asked what he meant by this, Uncle Andrew explained that when Grandmother was a little girl, every house had a piece of furniture called a whatnot that was filled to overflowing with things

that were almost never used. In fact, people like Grandmother who lived
in the Victorian Age wanted their whole houses to be like whatnots, filled
with every kind of useless, as well as useful, thing.

And then Uncle Andrew told John
and Lucy the story of Grandmother's house.

One day, along about 1880, Grandmother's father brought
home *another* marble statue. Her mother usually liked these presents very
much because in those days everyone wanted statues in the parlor. But
this time she had to say that there wasn't room for one more thing in their
old house. And that was why Grandmother's father went to the architect to talk about plans for the new house — the house that is Grandmother's
old house today.

The architect showed him many plans. And he started to draw the new one for Grandmother's father's house.

But because it was a time when people liked to copy things that had been done before, the architect said he would look back into the whole, long history of art to get ideas for the new house.

First, he looked back into the time called prehistoric, the stone age, when men who lived in caves painted on their rock walls. One of them painted a bison — so beautiful that it is hard to believe it was painted twenty thousand years before Christ was born.

The Cave Men in those days also made carvings from bone and the horns of reindeer. After the day's hunting, they sat around the fire at night to make the carvings and to look out the cave entrance to the sky and the stars.

Horse's Head carved in Reindeer Horn

It is interesting to look at the things they carved in those evenings so long ago. We still have some of them in museums today. There were dart throwers and other useful objects but there were also some carvings that were made just for the pleasure of carving them.

As time went on and the skill of the Cave Men increased, they also made pottery and decorated their jugs and other objects with spiral and geometric patterns.

Pottery from Neolithic Age

Dart Thrower carved in Reindeer Horn

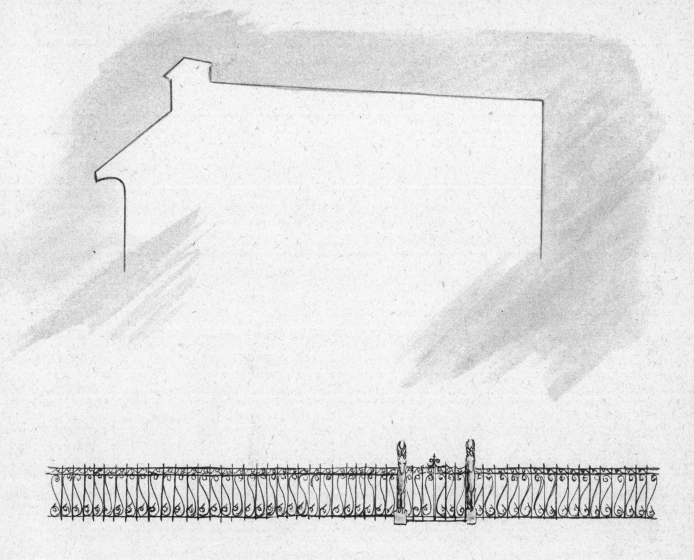

"Ah," said the architect after he had looked at the work of the Cave Men, "here we are! Just exactly what we want." He took the dart thrower and copied it for gate posts. Then he fitted the nice spirals on the pottery into a design for the long, iron fence.

Grandmother's father was very pleased to have a piece of his new house copied from things that were made so long ago.

They looked
next to Egypt three thousand years before Christ
lived. It seems now impossible to believe that
the Egyptians living so long before Christian
civilization began, had a civilization of their own
in many ways as advanced as our own. These
were the great days of Egyptian art — the days
of the pyramids and the wall paintings,
like this one of a Noble hunting from a
boat, or the one below of a slave farmer
driving flocks across a canal.

Cattle Fording a Canal

Noble Hunting from a boat

Khafre

Ceremonial Vase

Queen Nofretete

These were days of great kings and queens. Egyptians of the Old Kingdom carved this statue of Khafre, who built the Middle Pyramid and lived around 2800 B.C. Later, in the Empire, they carved Queen Nofretete, who, famed for her beauty, lived from 1375 to 1358 B.C. The Egyptians' art was so much a part of their life and the worship of their gods that the perfection of their creative works has seldom been surpassed.

Chapel of Pyramid of Sahure

The Egyptians originally built their great temples inside the Pyramids, which they made as houses for their gods. Later the temples often became separated from the pyramids. They used heavy columns and laid massive slabs of stone across the tops of the temples to form the roof. This is the Colonnaded Hall of the Chapel of the Pyramid of Sahure, 2735 B.C.

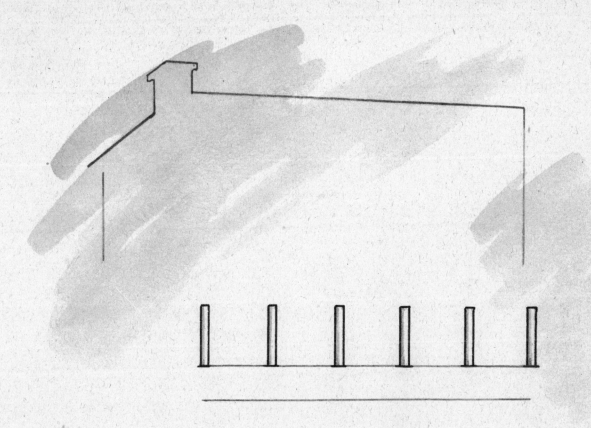

"I think I shall use Egyptian columns across the front of the house," said the architect, turning back from history to his plan. "But I don't so much care for the palm leaf capitals on the tops of the Egyptian columns. We'll find some others later that I think you will like better." So they took the columns from Egypt of about 3000 years before Christ and copied them for the 1880 house, and Grandmother's father approved.

Ashurbanipal Hunting

A Mede bringing a Tribute of Horses

At the time that the great art of ancient Egypt was beginning to decline and weaken there grew up to the east of Egypt in Asia in the valley of the Tigris and Euphrates rivers another civilization and another great art. Babylonian art began to develop (around 3000 B.C.) and became what we know as Babylonian-Assyrian Art, and at its height (around 900 to 600 B.C.) we know it as Assyrian. The warlike nature of the Babylonians and Assyrians shows in their art. These pictures show Assyrian sculpture from about 800 to 600 B.C.

Winged Figure

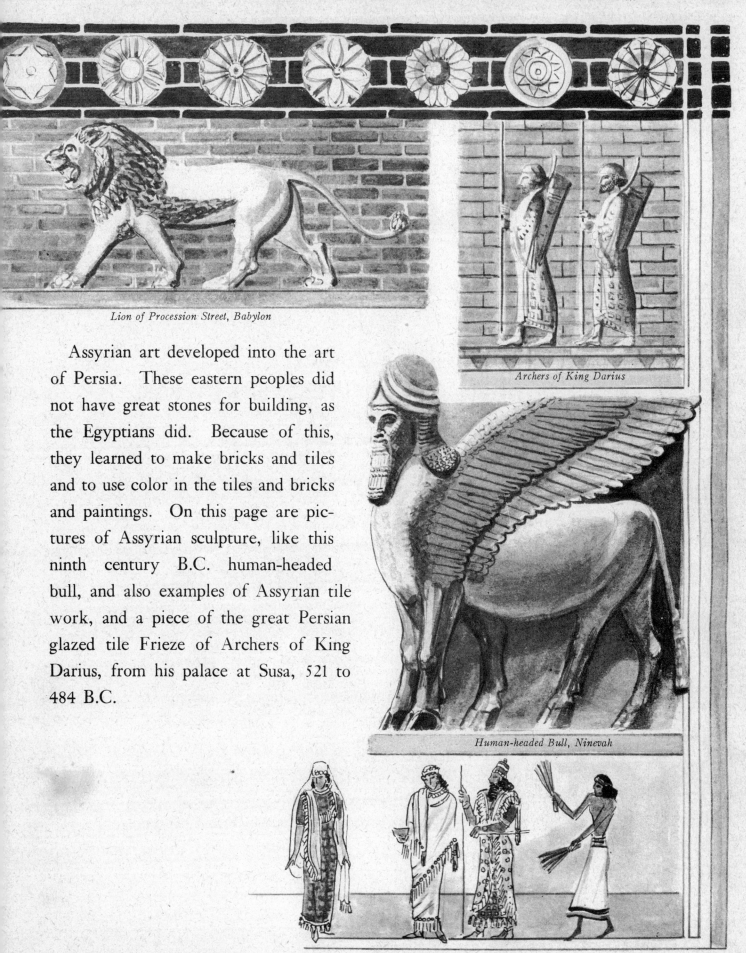

Lion of Procession Street, Babylon

Archers of King Darius

Human-headed Bull, Ninevah

Assyrian art developed into the art of Persia. These eastern peoples did not have great stones for building, as the Egyptians did. Because of this, they learned to make bricks and tiles and to use color in the tiles and bricks and paintings. On this page are pictures of Assyrian sculpture, like this ninth century B.C. human-headed bull, and also examples of Assyrian tile work, and a piece of the great Persian glazed tile Frieze of Archers of King Darius, from his palace at Susa, 521 to 484 B.C.

And because the Assyrians did not have heavy stones,
they developed the arch made of many stones fitted together. They also
built great, square towers, like those shown here in the Palace of Sargon II
at Khorsabad (Restored). They used these great towers for worship and
as lookouts and ramparts for the protection of their cities in wartime.

The architect of the 1880 house seemed to like the Babylonian, Assyrian, and Persian art and architecture very much. He put a great, square tower at one end of the house and copied the Assyrian arches to connect his Egyptian columns. Even before he reached the time of Christ in the history of art, the architect had borrowed enough to make his house a hodgepodge whatnot, but Grandmother's father liked it that way.

Bull Catching and Hunting Scenes.   Gold Cups from Vaphio

Octopus Vase

As far back as the Old Kingdom of Egypt, art had begun to develop on Crete and the islands of the beautiful Aegean Sea.   In those days, the island people were safe from invasion.   Ships were not equipped for extensive warfare, and attack from the air did not come until 1941.   Because they were a peaceful people, the Aegeans were able to develop pure design. They naturally looked for inspiration to the sea that surrounded them. They drew and painted the octopus and made him a beautiful, decorative design for their pottery vases.   They also painted fish and shells and other sea plants and creatures.   The greatest art of the Aegean was developed in Crete and reached its height about 1500 to 1300 B.C., which came during two periods — the Minoan, on the islands in the Aegean (3000 to 1400 B.C.) and the Mycenaean, on the mainland of Greece (1400–1100 B.C.)

Bull Fight Fresco

Flying Fish Fresco. Crete

This was the time that the great Palace of Minos in Knossos was built. The flying fishes are from a wall painting of this palace. Bull hunting and bull fighting were favorite sports and they are shown in the designs at the top of the page, one made for golden cups, the other painted on a wall (about 1500 B.C.) The beautiful gold and ivory snake goddess, which stands only about six and three-eighths inches high, is also from Crete.

Cretan Snake Goddess

The women who lived in the time of Minos wore bell shaped, flowered dresses like those they put on their snake goddess. This picture shows some of them filling ceremonial vases in the palace of King Minos at Knossos in Crete.

The architect looked back from the art history pages to his plan. "Let's take from the Aegean Islanders a beautiful, shell pattern that fits so neatly between our arches, and decorate their curves with a pattern from a Cretan lady's skirt," he said.

Uncle Andrew sighed. He didn't like to tell John and Lucy how Grandmother's father's architect took bits and pieces of the designs of the Aegeans for his hodgepodge house.

But it was what Grandmother's father wanted and what architects in 1880 liked, so there was nothing to do but to turn and see what they would add next.

Chinese art and civilization is as old as that of Egypt, though we do not have as many fine pieces of ancient Chinese art in our museums. This is because China has been less touched by the western world than any other great nation. Chinese art is as mysterious and beautiful as its age-old country. As the Aegeans turned naturally to the growing things of the sea that surrounded them, so the Chinese turned to nature for their inspiration. They carved great mystical beasts in stone and jade, and made paintings on paper like this Tiger, below, of the Sung Dynasty, 960–1280 A.D.

Tiger

They painted their mountains and took patterns from leaves and flowers. They made likenesses of their gods and goddesses like Bodhisattva shown here (T'ang Dynasty, 618–907 A.D.) and built temples in which to worship them. Their art and civilization is divided into dynasties named for their rulers. The bronze vessel shown below dates to about 1000 B.C.

Bodhisattva

Bronze Vessel

Stone Lion

Because the Chinese loved nature, they surrounded their temples with gardens, with trees and flowers, and streams crossed by little bridges. They placed their great, carved, stone images in the gardens as well as in the temples. This stone lion was made in the Han Dynasty around 700 B.C.

"We will take a great, stone lion from the Chinese who lived before Christ and let him guard the entrance to our 1880 house," said the architect, very pleased with himself. "And I think we should also have a Chinese tree for our garden."

Grandmother's father agreed. He had been to China on a Grand Tour and he loved what he called their "out-of-door art."

Uncle Andrew stopped for a moment to explain that Greek art, which came next, also flourished before the time of Christ. It really grew out of the Aegean art and reached its peak about 420 B.C. Greece in those days was a nation of small states, not unlike our own, except that these Greek states were really cities and the country immediately around them. It was natural that these cities, like Athens and Corinth and Sparta, should develop different styles in art and architecture, since they competed with one another in every possible way.

Doric

The Greek city states came to adopt for themselves one of three "orders" of architecture: Doric, which was simple and low with sturdy columns; Corinthian, which was more elaborate and ornate with delicate columns; and Ionic, which was somewhere between the simple Doric and elaborate Corinthian styles, with its well-proportioned scrolls.

The Greeks were great vase makers and painters. They decorated their pottery with scenes of everyday life, sports, games, chariot races. They also used decorative animals and flowers and spirals. The famous François Vase was made in the sixth century B.C.

François Vase

Ionic

Corinthian

...eze of Horses from the Parthenon, now in British Museum

The Greeks owed much to the older arts of Egypt and the Aegean islands. They made statues of bronze and marble and stone in honor of their athletes and their gods and goddesses. And like the Egyptians, they roofed their temples with massive slabs of stone.

The fifth century B.C. was the great period of Greek art and civilization and the greatest sculptors were Myron, Phidias, and Praxiteles.

Discobolus by Myron

Charioteer of Delphi

29

The Parthenon

Athena Lemnia by Phidias?

The Athenians built a great Doric temple called the Parthenon to their goddess, Athena. This temple has a most beautiful frieze, which goes around the entire building in the space between the roof and the tops of the inner row of columns. It also has two pediments, the triangular spaces at each short end of the building, which are also heavily sculptured. Today, although in ruins, this temple still stands on the Acropolis, the hill which overlooks the great city of the ancient Greeks.

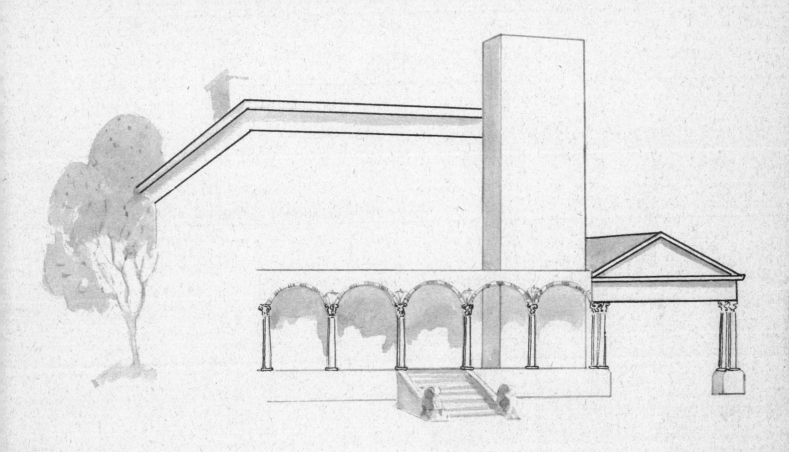

"It seems an odd thing to us," said Uncle Andrew, "that Grandmother's father's architect should have taken bits and pieces of Greek art and mixed them with all the other bits and pieces that went into his house. Greek art of all others was designed to belong to itself and its time. But there it is, and, of course, Great-grandfather loved the Greek line of the roof, the pediment of the porte-cochere (the carriage entrance on the side), and the Corinthian capitals to his Egyptian columns."

We come next to Roman art. Grandmother's father and his architect both admired this very much because they had both been to Rome and had seen the remains of ancient Roman buildings and works of art for themselves. The Romans conquered the Greeks (about 150 B.C.) because the Greeks had come into a period of weakness and decline. The Roman conquerors copied the Greeks and imitated much of their art. But they did not always copy exactly because they loved fancy things in the same way that the 1880 whatnot people did.

*Wall Painting
Birds and Fountain*

*Wall Painting
Cupid Riding a Crab*

Roman sculptors made many statues of their great Caesar Augustus and other emperors, statesmen, and warriors. They tried always to make these statues realistic with every line and wrinkle in the faces accurate.

Caracalla

Caesar Augustus

Temple of the Sibyl

Arch of Titus

The Romans were greater engineers and architects than sculptors and painters. Their aqueducts and bridges and their baths with plumbing, and even heated water, amaze scientists today. They were the first to build round buildings and to make much use of the arch as a monument.

These arches were built so that the soldiers, returning victorious from the wars, could march underneath and celebrate their triumphs.

The Greek cornice (under the main roof) and pediment of the 1880 house were decorated with fancy Roman ornaments, garlands and elaborate patterns that delighted Grandmother's father and his architect.

Mosaic — The good Shepherd

Mosaic — Empress Theodora

About four centuries after the birth of Christ the Romans became Christians, and Roman art came to be called Christian art because it was so much influenced by the life of Christ and the stories of the Old Testament. As the great Roman Empire grew more and more powerful, Roman warriors pushed north into Britain and east along the Mediterranean. So it was that when Constantine became emperor in 324 A.D., he moved the capital of the Roman Empire from Rome to Byzantium on the eastern end of the Mediterranean Sea. He called it Constantinople — the city that we now know as Istanbul in Turkey.

Byzantine Column and Capital

Byzantine Reliefs

Constantine was the first Christian emperor. He so greatly admired Byzantine art that he had it copied for his churches in all parts of the Empire. The art of Byzantium owed much to that of Persia, of Babylonia, and Assyria. The Byzantines made mosaics, for which they used tiny, inlaid precious stones to make decorations and portraits. They loved color, spirals, filagrees, and intricate carvings. When Justinian, who came several hundred years after Constantine, was emperor, many portraits of his wife, Theodora, were made. On this page is a picture of the carving of the Empress Eudosia, wife of Romanus IV, Emperor of Constantinople, which was made in the sixth century, B.C.

Ivory Carving — Empress Eudosia

Santa Sophia

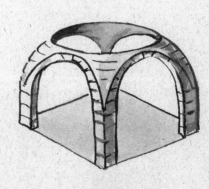

It was Justinian who was responsible for the building of Santa Sophia (532 to 537 A.D.) in Constantinople. His architects were the first to discover how to put a round dome on a square building, as the pictures show.

Of course, great-grandfather's architect chose the dome to copy from the Byzantine Romans. He placed it on top of the square tower of the Assyrians and added a bay window with a rounded top like a half dome. Great-grandfather loved these elaborate touches and grew more and more fond of his house.

"Before we turn to Gothic art," said Uncle Andrew, "we should remember our history. Rome fell in 476 A.D. Its collapse was followed by what is called the Romanesque period of architecture in Italy, France, and Germany up to the end of the 12th century. The period after the fall of Rome has come to be known as the *Dark Ages*. Rome had been the great, stern power that held lawlessness in check. When Rome fell, law and order fell with it. Art and literature, civilization itself, were kept alive only by the church. Monks, safe in their monasteries, copied the literature of the past and made beautiful decorative illustrations that we call illuminations."

The Reaper

Chartres

Notre Dame (Paris)

Reims

But in the Dark Ages, the way was prepared for the great rebirth in the arts of civilization, which began in the 12th and 13th centuries and reached its height in the 14th and 15th centuries. The art of the 12th and 15th centuries came to be known as *Gothic*. This was the time of the great cathedrals in France, Germany, England and, later, in Italy.

Stained glass windows

Gargoyle

Canterbury   *York*   *Cologne*

In England,
Roman begin-
nings had been fol-
lowed by Anglo-Saxon,
to become Norman after
the Conquest in 1066. In
Canterbury, for example, Nor-
man beginnings were added to and enlarged upon in the
Gothic period. The delicate spires and the elaborations of
detail, as in the gargoyles of Notre Dame in Paris were char-
acteristic of the Gothic. The beautiful stained glass windows
show the influence of Byzantine art on what was then the
"western world." All the people helped in the building of
the great cathedrals. Stone masons, artists, craftsmen —
each individual — gave something of himself to his work.
Often the small carvings in stone or wood, like this Virgin
of Amiens in France, were the work of local artists.

Gilded Virgin

Notre Dame in Paris

It is hard for us to realize that these cathedrals took more than a man's life-time to build so that the work was handed down from father to son. In spite of this, the master hand that made the plan was so skillful that the cathedrals have never been surpassed in purity of design and in beauty. Notre Dame in Paris, started in 1163, is one of the best known and best loved cathedrals. The spires were never added to the towers, but it is a splendid example of Gothic art.

Grandmother's father watched the architect add stained glass to the bay windows and a small round window to the tower. This round window, like the ones in the Gothic churches, he called a "rose window" because that is what the Gothic cathedral round windows are called. He also gave the tower and the balcony some Gothic touches. Great-grandfather was much impressed, and his house was nearly done.

Flight into Egypt, by Giotto

St. Francis Preaching to the Birds by Giotto

Mona Lisa by Leonardo da Vinci

Leonardo da Vinci flying one of his model airplanes

While cathedrals were being built, the art of painting was developing from the delicate miniature illustrations of the illuminated manuscripts made in the monasteries to the larger wall painting. Giotto, in his famous murals done about 1300 in the little hill town of Assisi in Italy, was the first to step away from the stiff figures of the miniatures and one of the first painters to give his people life-like form and color. Gradually, painting and sculpture developed until, in the 15th century, came the full flowering of the period known as the Renaissance because it was the rebirth of classical forms after the dark days of the Middle Ages. Artists began to look back to the Greeks and the Romans, and so, once again, to nature, for their inspiration.

St. George
by Donatello

David by
Michelangelo

Giotto and the men who followed him paved the way for Leonardo da Vinci and Michelangelo, the two great figures of the Italian Renaissance. Leonardo was a scientist, as well as painter and sculptor. Many of the ideas which he wrote down in his notebooks were so far ahead of his time that they have not been developed until very recently in our own day. Michelangelo was a great painter and sculptor who followed Leonardo. His murals in the Sistine Chapel and his *David*, also in Florence, are considered by many his finest work. There were many other sculptors and painters, whose names we all know, in this time of great flowering of art.

Bambino by Andrea della Robbia

Andrea della Robbia developed the art of making figurines and portrait reliefs in terra cotta.

Cantora by Luca della Robbia

Colleoni
by Verrochio

45

Farnese Palace

As the Renaissance progressed, architecture also reflected the return to classic Greece and Rome for inspiration. The Gothic lines were smoothed and straightened and simplified. But many of the Gothic touches remained. This is the Farnese Palace (1520–1580) in Rome — classic in design and with a variety of arches and pediments. The top story is supposed to have been designed by Michelangelo in 1546.

After looking at the drawing of the Farnese Palace, Grandmother's father had an idea about the windows of his house. He asked the architect to add some rounded and some square pediments and to make some arched and some square window openings. So the architect looked to the Renaissance for last touches and was delighted. He had been looking for some way to "fancy up" his windows.

The influence of the Renaissance in Italy spread northwards in Europe. The Van Eycks in Flanders discovered the use of oil for mixing paints in the 15th century.

From the time of the Renaissance, art flourished throughout Europe and in England. The names of great artists stand out — Hogarth, Durer, El Greco, Rembrandt, Vermeer — but for the most part, the centuries up to the 19th were years of lesser art and lesser architecture.

Mme. Récamier by David

In 1755, a discovery was made that greatly influenced art and architecture. People digging at Pompeii in Italy uncovered an untouched town, just as it had been in the first century after the birth of Christ when Roman art had closely copied that of the Greeks. The old Pompeii had been preserved almost unharmed because it had perished in an eruption of Vesuvius, a nearby volcano. Hot lava had poured down on the old town, snuffing out its life and sealing it for a thousand years. People in the 18th century travelled to Pompeii to see the diggings, books were written about them, and the Graeco-Roman art of old Pompeii was copied everywhere.

Arc de L'Etoile

Fashionable ladies wore dresses of the period. Furniture was copied from that found in Pompeii. In Paris, the Pantheon was built in Graeco-Roman style, and in 1806 a Roman triumphal arch was built to celebrate Napoleon's victories. In the United States in 1832 Horatio Greenough made a marble statue of George Washington that made him look very much like a Roman senator.

The Pantheon

George Washington by Greenough

"There," said the architect, "that brings us up to our own 1880. We can put a Pompeiian fountain in the front yard and then I think we have everything."

Grandmother's father was completely satisfied. He ordered the architect to build the house exactly as he had planned it.

And here is the house finished at last.

Not many years after it was built, Grandmother grew up and married, and her father gave her the "mansion" as he called it for a wedding present.

"No wonder Grandmother likes it so much," said Lucy.

"Of course she likes the house," said Uncle Andrew, "but any good architect today would say that it is dreadful. Inside and outside it's a what-not house."

"Architects today like what they call 'functional' houses," Uncle Andrew went on, "houses that are planned for the needs of the people who live in them. Everything has a use; often the furniture is built in so that it, too, becomes a part of the house.

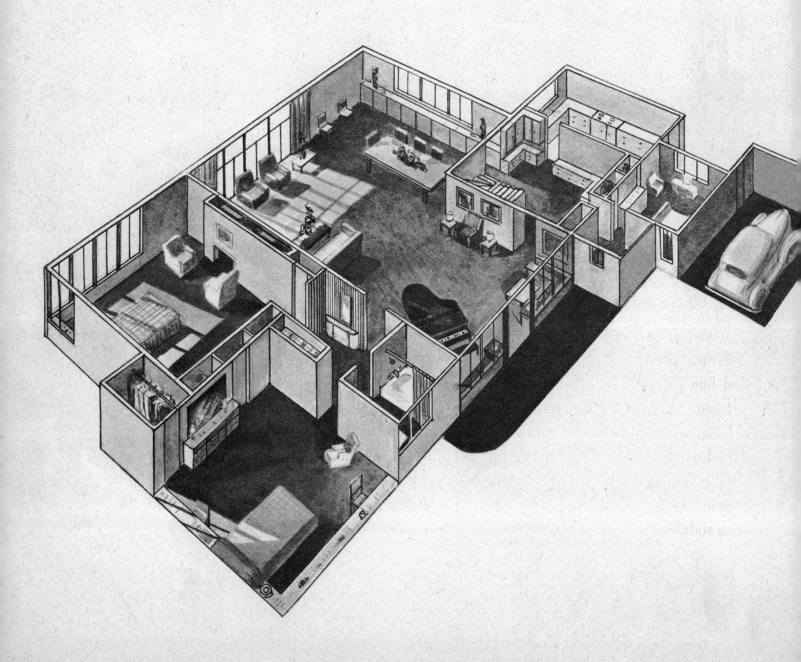

"The outside of such a house is simply a covering made to fit over the plan but made to fit neatly and with a sense of design and order and plan.

"You may not like these houses," Uncle Andrew said, "but you would like to live in them and play in them much more than in Grandmother's house because they are made to live in and play in — not to be museums."

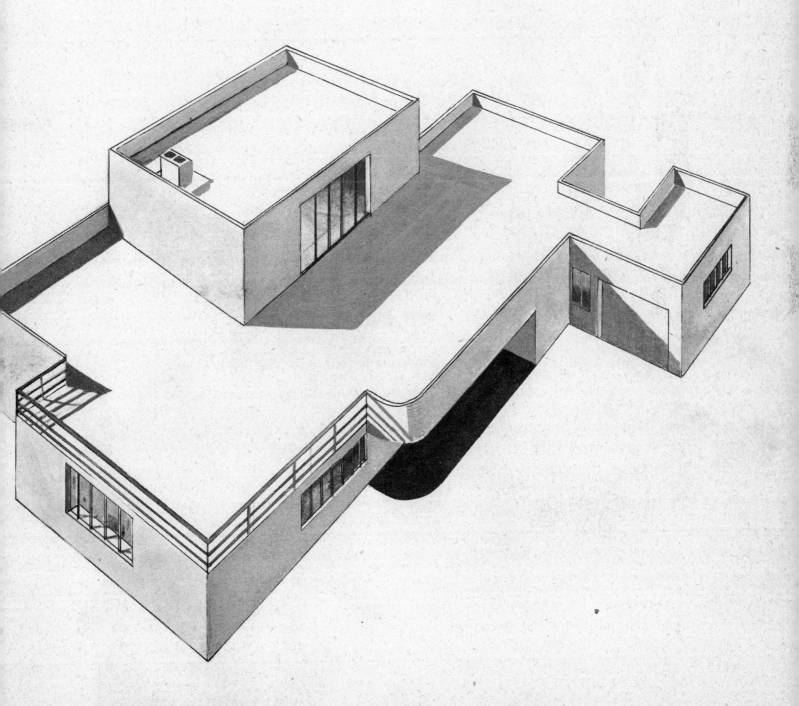

"The Whatnot Age did something to sculpture and painting, too. Sculpture became fussy, trying so hard to tell a story that the feeling of the stone or the bronze or the marble was lost. There was no beauty of form and no strength. It was Archipenko, a Russian, who first, in about 1913 began to simplify and reduce sculpture to its elemental forms. Other great sculptors since then have given back to sculpture its primitive strength and character. Men like Carl Milles, a Swede, can do a piece of sculpture, like this Boar Hunt, that is pure design and pattern as easily and as well as they can design more traditional recognizable subjects. But they have cured themselves of the fussy weaknesses of the Whatnot Age.

Florentine Singer by Du Bois

Statuette by Archipenko

Boar Hunt by Carl Milles

Spring by Corot

Two Girls Reading by Picasso

"Grandmother's generation thought Corot the greatest painter of all time. Today the weaknesses of Corot and the Impressionists who followed him have been pointed out by painters like Picasso, who could make his fundamental pattern so sure and so strong that it could stand as painting, even without any detail to make it a pretty picture. He gave back to painting the color and rhythm and feeling of form that the Victorian painters had lost."

Madonna of the Chair by Raphael

The old masters painted in strong, rhythmic shapes. If the detail and finish were removed from any great painting, the pattern would be very like Picasso's. We can, for example, put a piece of tracing paper over Raphael's *Madonna of the Chair* and trace the areas of color and light and dark, which are what we see when we shut our eyes to the picture-story. What we get when we do this is a dark outline, not unlike the outlines that Picasso might make. Then, if we fill in the color, we have the same kind of pattern picture that we saw in Picasso's *Two Girls Reading*.

Uncle Andrew smiled at John's and Lucy's surprise. He knew they had another question —

"What," they said, "will happen when we grow up? Will your modern house be as bad to the new architects as Grandmother's house is to you?" Uncle Andrew stopped smiling. He didn't quite like the idea that anyone, ever, might not like his house. But he tried to answer wisely.

"No one knows," he said, "what tomorrow will bring. With World War II and the science of aviation have come new materials that we call *plastics*. Perhaps when you grow up we will all live in plastic houses. Already we have plastic sculpture and furniture.

"Out of the war and the new sciences will come new patterns and shapes and ideas for the painting and the sculpture and the buildings of the future."

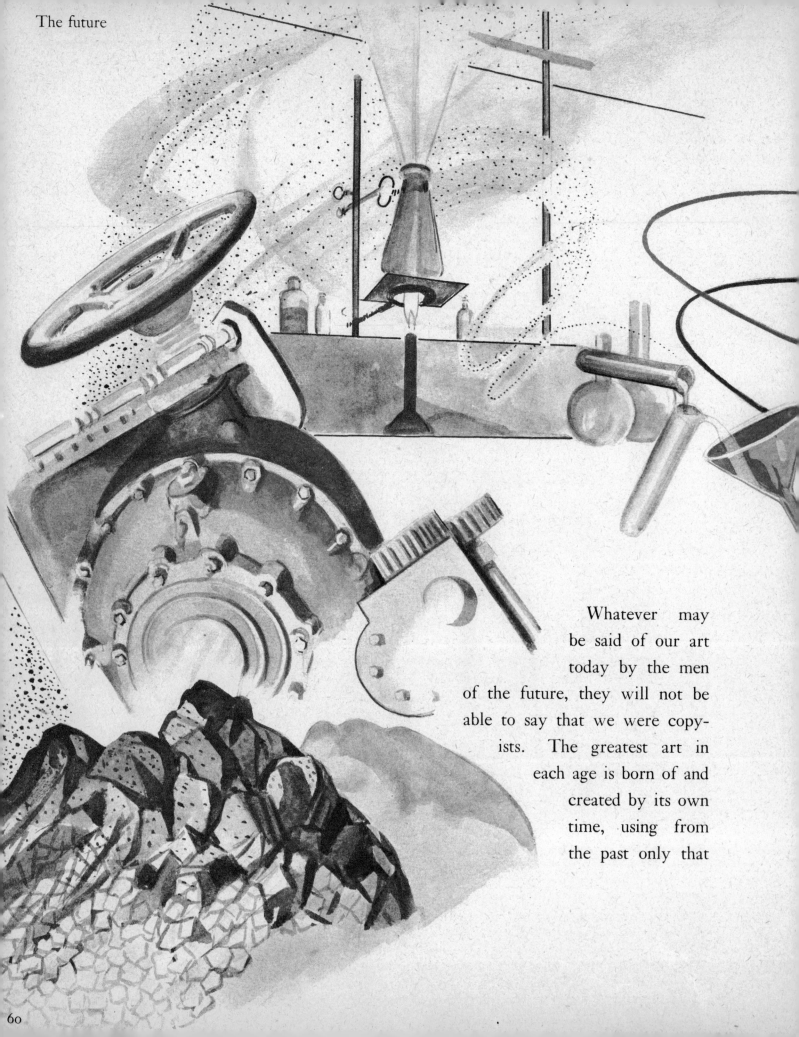

Whatever may be said of our art today by the men of the future, they will not be able to say that we were copyists. The greatest art in each age is born of and created by its own time, using from the past only that

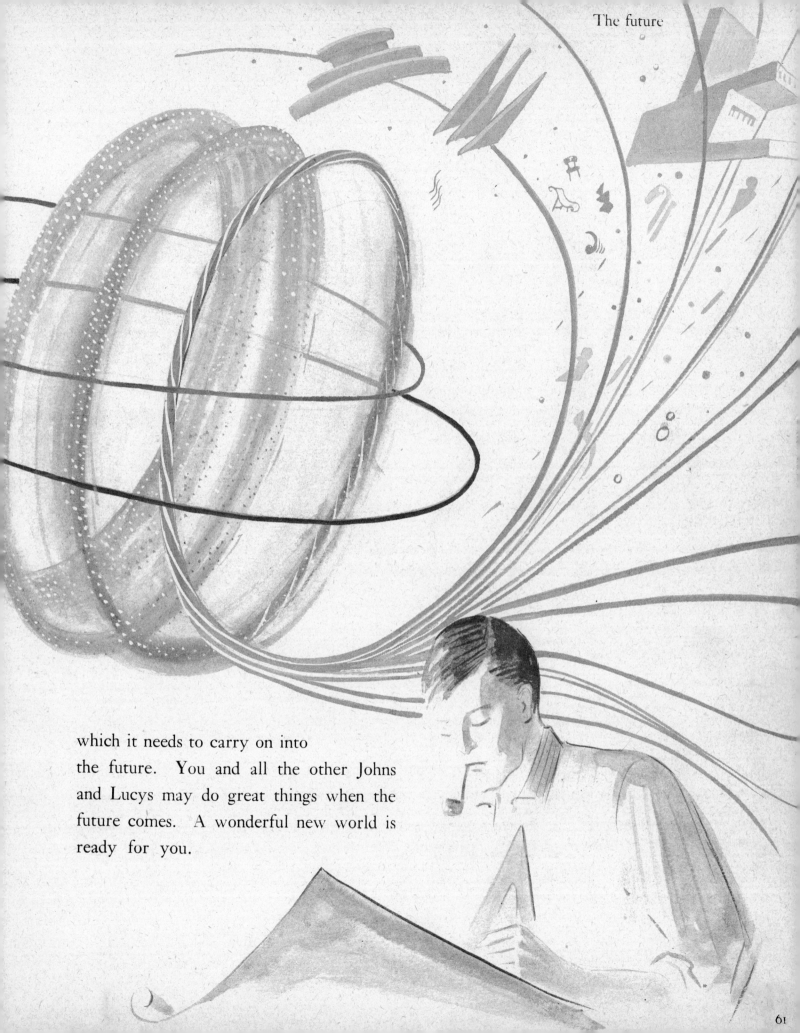

which it needs to carry on into
the future. You and all the other Johns
and Lucys may do great things when the
future comes. A wonderful new world is
ready for you.